Exploring Antarctica

Continents of the World Geography Series

By
MICHAEL KRAMME, Ph.D.

ISBN 10-digit: 1-58037-224-4
13-digit: 978-1-58037-224-4

Printing No. CD-1570

Mark Twain Media, Inc., Publishers
Distributed by Carson-Dellosa Publishing Company, Inc.

Table of Contents

The Continents

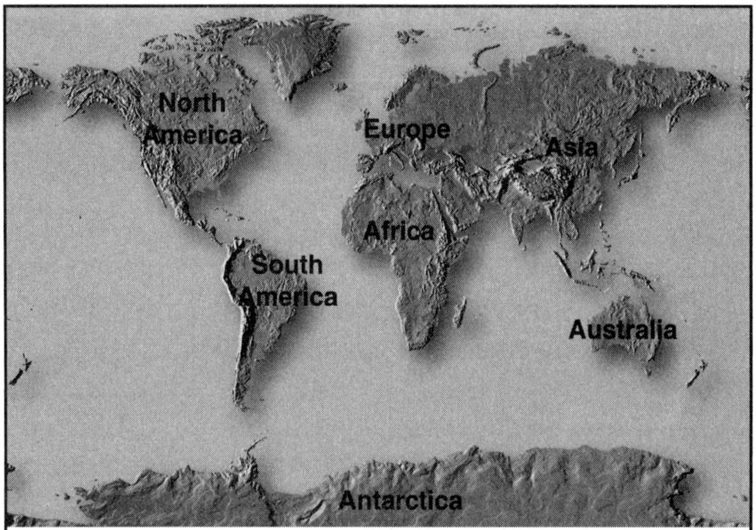

The Continents Today

A continent is a large landmass completely or mostly surrounded by water. Geographers list seven continents: North America, South America, Europe, Asia, Africa, Australia, and Antarctica. Greenland and the India-Pakistan area are sometimes referred to as "subcontinents." Madagascar and the Seychelles Islands are often called "microcontinents." The island groups in the Pacific Ocean are called "Oceania," but they are not considered a continent.

The continents make up just over 29 percent of the earth's surface. They occupy about 57,100,000 square miles (148,000,000 sq. km). More than 65 percent of the land area is in the Northern Hemisphere.

HOW WERE THE CONTINENTS FORMED?

For many years, Europeans believed the continents were formed by a catastrophe or series of catastrophes, such as floods, earthquakes, and volcanoes. In 1596, a Dutch mapmaker, Abraham Ortelius, noted that the Americas' eastern coasts and the western coasts of Europe and Africa looked as if they fit together. He proposed that once they had been joined but later were torn apart.

Many years later, a German named Alfred Lothar Wegener published a book in which he explained his theory of the "**Continental Drift**." Wegener, like Ortelius, believed that the earth originally had one super continent. He named it **Pangaea** from the Greek word meaning "all lands." He believed that the large landmass was a lighter rock that floated on a heavier rock, like ice floats on water.

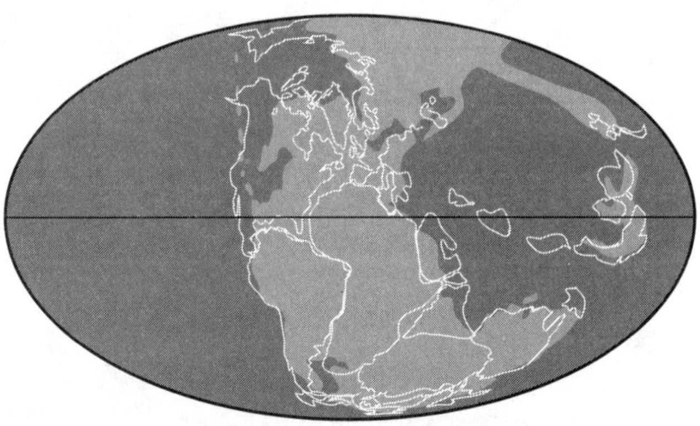

Wegener's theoretical continent, Pangaea, during the Permian Age (white outlines indicate current continents)

Wegener's theory stated that the landmasses were still moving at a rate of about one yard each century. Wegener believed that Pangaea existed in the Permian Age. Then Pangaea slowly divided into two continents, the upper part, **Laurasia**, and the lower, **Gondwanaland**, during the Triassic Age.

By the Jurassic Age, the landmasses had moved into what we could recognize as the seven continents, although they were still located near each other. Eventually, the continents "drifted" to their present locations.

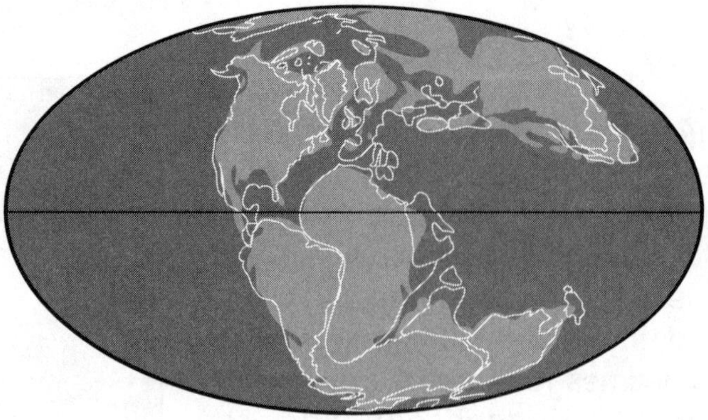

Landmasses during the Jurassic Age

Most scientists had been in agreement on the continental drift theory until researchers in the 1960s discovered several major mountain ranges on the ocean floor. These mountains suggested that the earth's crust consists of about 20 slabs or **plates**.

These discoveries led to a new theory, "**Plate Tectonics**," which has become more popular. This theory suggests that these plates move a few inches each year. In some places the plates are moving apart, while in others the plates are colliding or scraping against each other.

Scientists also discovered that most volcanoes and earthquakes occur along the boundaries of the various plates. They hope that further study will help them increase their understanding of Earth's story.

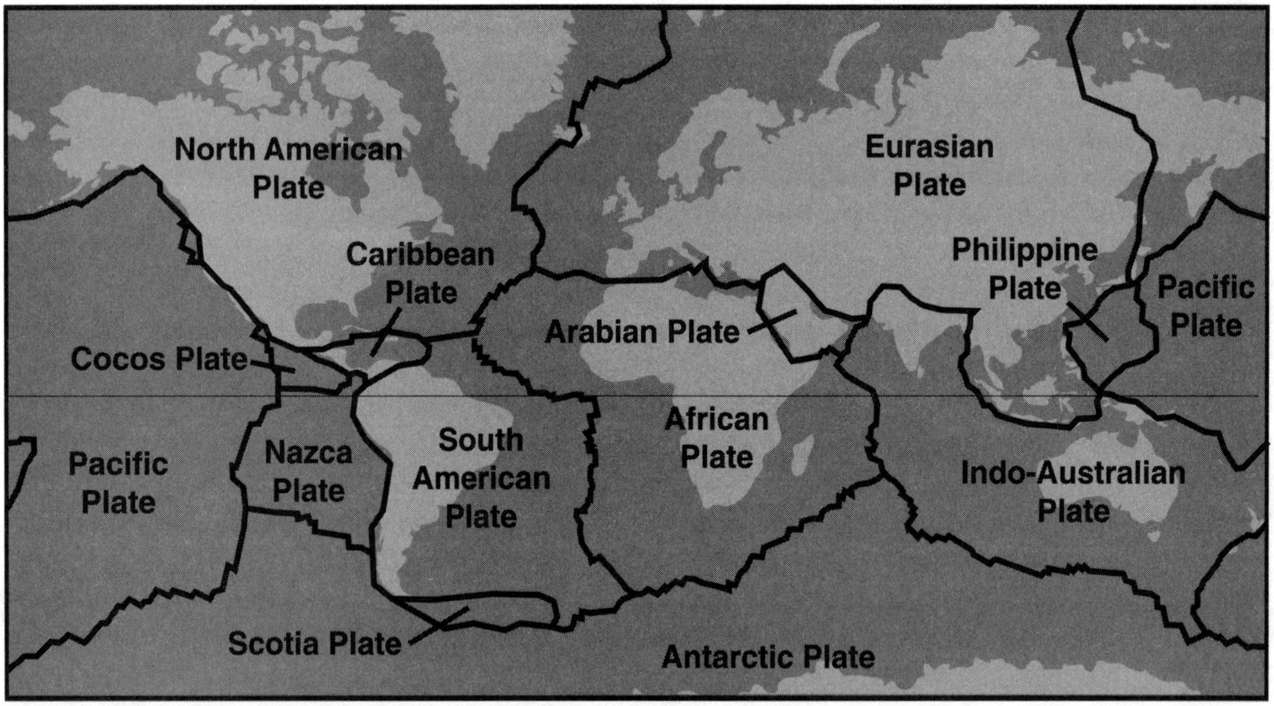

The Tectonic Plates

Name: ______________________________ Date: ______________

Questions for Consideration

1. What is a continent? ______________________________
____
2. The continents make up what percentage of the earth's surface?
____
3. What was the name of Wegener's theory?
____
4. What is the name of the newer theory that replaced Wegener's?
____
5. What two natural happenings occur near the boundaries of the plates?
____

Map Project

On the map below, label all seven of the continents.

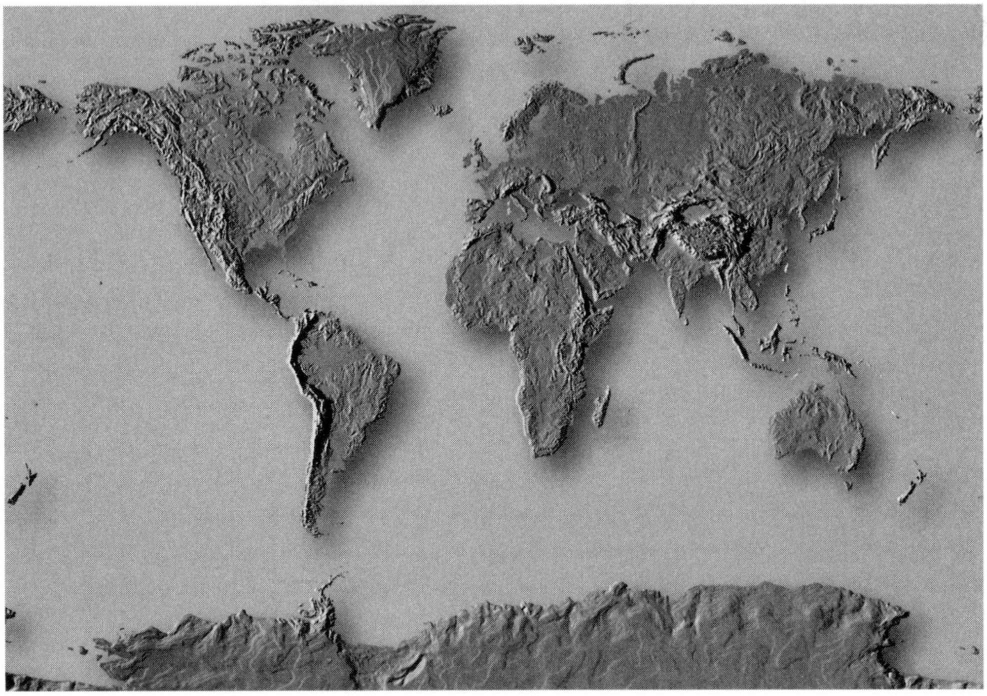

Name: ____ Date: ____________________

Outline Map of Antarctica

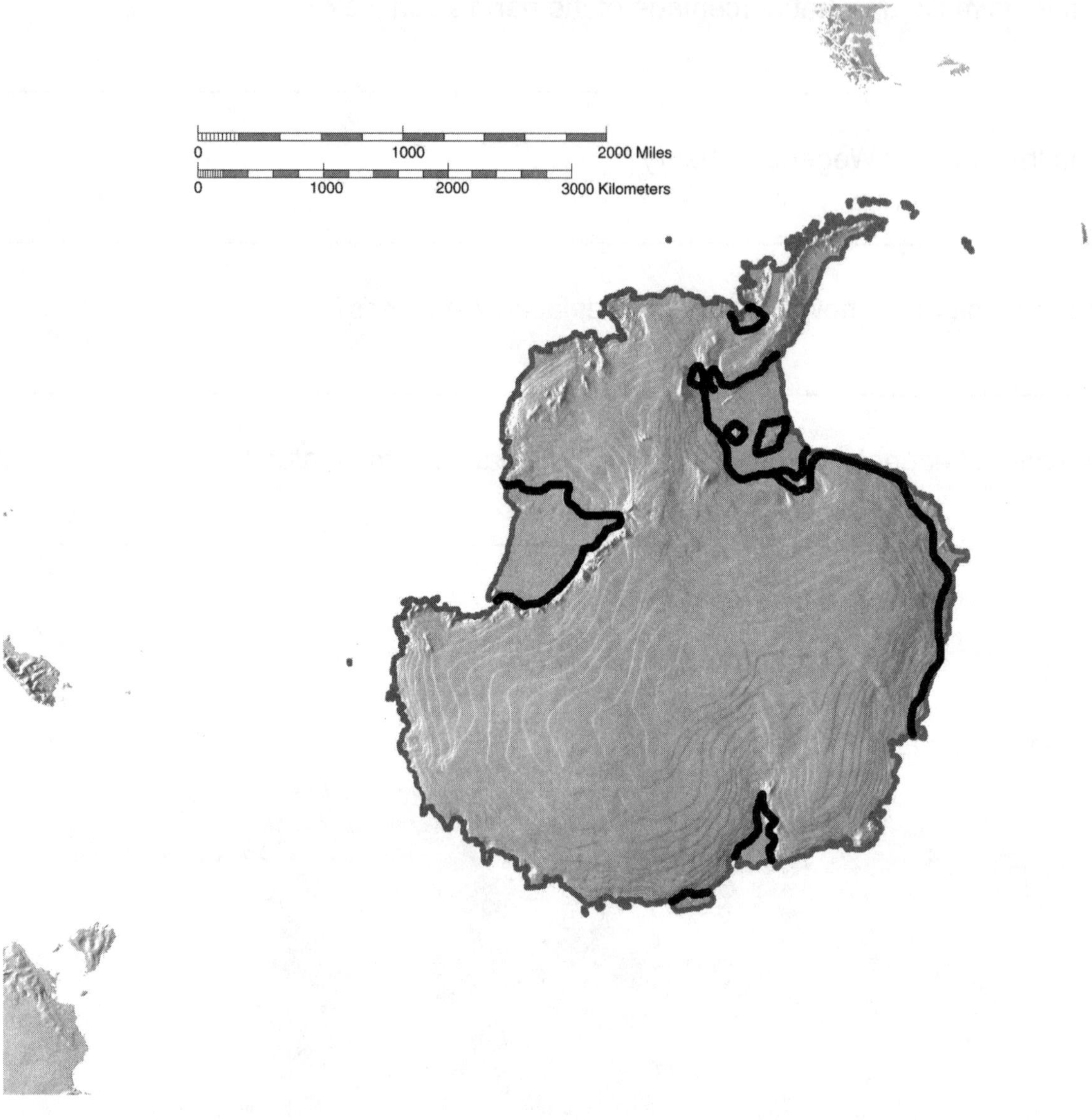

*Black outlines indicate coastline covered by ice shelves.

The Continent of Antarctica

Antarctica is the world's southernmost continent. It surrounds the South Pole, which is the earth's most southern point.

Its name means "opposite the Arctic." The Arctic is the earth's northernmost region. Antarctica is the fifth-largest continent. It is larger than Australia or Europe. It is slightly less than one and one-half the size of the United States.

The Transantarctic Mountains divide the continent into two regions, West Antarctica and East Antarctica.

Because of Antarctica's severe weather, it is the only continent that does not have any permanent residents. Twenty-nine nations send scientists to several research stations located on the continent. The population of the research stations varies from about 3,500 in the summer to 1,000 in the winter. In recent years, tourists have begun to visit the continent.

It is bitterly cold and almost completely covered by a huge sheet of ice. The ice is often two miles thick near the center of the continent; it then thins out towards the coastline. This sheet contains about 90 percent of the world's ice. Below the ice, the land area of Antarctica is about the size of Australia. Just over two percent of its area is exposed land. Much of the land that is exposed is mountaintops.

As snow falls in the central region, it forces the ice sheet to move very slowly toward the coastlines. Often, when the ice reaches the water's edge, it floats, creating an "ice shelf." Antarctica has several ice shelves. The two largest are the Ross Ice Shelf and the Ronne Ice Shelf. The Ross Ice Shelf is about 4,000 feet (1,219 m) thick in places. Often, pieces break off the ice shelves and form icebergs.

Antarctica is surrounded by water, including the southern parts of the Atlantic, Pacific, and Indian Oceans. Sometimes, the waters off Antarctica's coast are referred to as the Antarctic Ocean or the Southern Ocean. Also along its coasts are the Amundsen, Ross, and Weddell Seas.

Antarctica is approximately 600 miles (1,000 km) from South America, 2,500 miles (4,000 km) from Africa, and 1,600 miles (2,500 km) from Australia.

Antarctica is the world's highest continent. Its average elevation is over 6,500 feet (2,000 m) above sea level. Its highest point is Vinson Massif which is 16,864 feet (5,140 m) high; its lowest point is on the Southern Ocean at zero feet (sea level).

The Transantarctic Mountains divide the continent into two regions, West Antarctica and East Antarctica.

Name: ______________________ Date: ______________

Questions for Consideration

1. What does the name "Antarctica" mean?

____

2. What mountains divide Antarctica into two regions?

____

3. What is the population of Antarctica in the summer?

____

4. Which continent is closest to Antarctica?

____

5. What is the highest point in Antarctica?

____

Map Project

Using an atlas or globe and the outline map of Antarctica (located on page 4), label the following:

Bodies of Water:	**Land Features:**
Amundsen Sea	Queen Maud Land (Dronning Maud Land)
Atlantic Ocean	Ronne Ice Shelf
Indian Ocean	Ross Ice Shelf
Pacific Ocean	South Pole
Ross Sea	Victoria Land
Weddell Sea	Wilkes Land

DID YOU KNOW?

Scientists recorded the world's coldest temperature, 128.6 degrees below zero (Fahrenheit), in Antarctica.

Antarctica's Climate

All of Antarctica's climates are cold. However, there are differences between the regions of the continent and the seasons of the year.

The temperature varies depending upon the season, latitude, elevation, and distance from the ocean.

Antarctica is the coldest place in the world. Its average temperature is about 20° colder than at the similar latitude in the northern arctic region.

The average summer temperatures along the coast are about 32°F (0°C). In the continent's interior, the summer temperatures average between -4° to -31°F (-20° to -35°C). The average winter temperatures stay below -40°F (-40°C).

The world's lowest temperature ever recorded was -128.6°F (-89°C). It was recorded in 1983 at the Russian Vostok Station. The world's lowest temperatures are in August.

Winds make it feel even colder. Commonwealth Bay is the world's windiest place. Winds often reach between 50 to 90 miles (80–145 km) per hour for several days. Wind gusts of over 120 miles (193 km) per hour are common during blizzards.

West Antarctica is warmer than East Antarctica because it has a lower elevation. The west coast of the Antarctic Peninsula has the mildest climates; in January, the temperature rises above freezing.

The interior region of Antarctica has almost constant daylight in the summer and darkness in the winter. Around December 21, most of the continent has a complete day of light; around June 21, it has a day of complete darkness.

Antarctica receives very little precipitation—it is the world's driest continent. Most of the precipitation is snow or ice. During the warm season, rain falls occasionally in the coastal regions. The coast receives an average of 10 to 20 inches (25 to 51 cm) each year. The interior receives less than 2 inches (5 cm) of precipitation each year.

In 1985, a hole in the ozone layer over Antarctica was first discovered. Each year between August and October, this ozone layer thins out. Since the ozone layer protects the earth from harmful ultraviolet radiation, this discovery concerns scientists. Scientists fear that the additional radiation will change Antarctica's ecological system and may affect the food chain of the continent's fish and other marine life. The size of the hole has been increasing. This has convinced many nations to reduce the use of chemicals that harm the ozone layer.

Name: ______________________________ Date: ______________

Questions for Consideration

1. What was the lowest temperature ever recorded?

____

2. Where is Antarctica's and the world's windiest place?

____

3. When does Antarctica have 24 hours of darkness?

____

4. How much rain does the interior of Antarctica receive each year?

____

5. When was the hole in the ozone layer first discovered?

____

Temperature

Temperature is recorded on two different scales, Farhenheit and Celsius.
To convert from Fahrenheit to Celsius, subtract 32° and divide by 1.8.
To convert from Celsius to Fahrenheit, multiply by 1.8 and add 32°.

Convert the following temperatures:

° Fahrenheit to °Celsius

1. -238° F = _______°C
2. 32° F = _______°C
3. 86°F = _______°C
4. 122°F = _______°C
5 203°F = _______°C

° Celsius to °Fahrenheit

6. 40°C = _______°F
7. 23.3°C = _______°F
8. 4.44°C = _______°F
9. 10°C = _______°F
10. -92°C = _______°F

DID YOU KNOW?

Since Antarctica is in the Southern Hemisphere, its seasons are the reverse of those in the Northern Hemisphere. January and February are the warmest months, and July and August are the coldest.

Antarctica's Ice

Over 95 percent of Antarctica is covered with ice. This ice comes in many forms.

A huge ice sheet covers most of the continent. An **ice sheet** is a thick layer of ice on top of a land mass. Antarctica's ice sheet is over two miles (3 km) thick in many places.

The ice sheet also makes Antarctica the world's highest continent. The ice sheet has an average thickness of 7,090 feet (2,160 m).

Antarctica's ice sheet contains about 90 percent of the world's ice. This is about 68 percent of the earth's fresh water.

About ten percent of Antarctica's ice cover consists of ice shelves. An **ice shelf** is a large floating piece of permanent ice. It is anchored to the land but extends over water.

The largest is the Ross Ice Shelf. It was named for British explorer James C. Ross. It is almost as large as the state of Texas. It is about 4,000 feet (1,219 m) thick in some places. Other major Antarctic ice shelves include the Amery, Filchner, Larsen, and Ronne.

Glaciers cover parts of both the ice sheet and ice shelves. **Glaciers** are moving masses of ice and come in many sizes. The largest glacier is the Lambert Glacier. It is 248 miles (399 km) long. Most glaciers are slow-moving. The fastest-moving glacier is the Shirase. It travels just over one mile (1.6 km) per year.

Glaciers are formed over hundreds of years. As new snow falls in the Antarctic region, it presses older snow into the ice. As the new ice is formed, it moves slowly from the interior of the continent toward the coastal regions. Glaciers move by the force of gravity and because of the added weight of more ice and snow.

Icebergs are floating masses of ice. They are formed when parts of glaciers reach the edge of land or an ice shelf or when parts of the ice shelf itself break off into the water. Icebergs have many sizes and shapes. The largest one recorded was over 200 miles (322 km) long and 60 miles (97 km) wide.

Most of an iceberg is below the water's surface. Only ten to 15 percent of the ice appears above the water's surface. Antarctica's icebergs drift westward around the continent and northward until they melt in warmer waters.

Pack ice is also common along the shores of the continent. Freezing seawater makes **pack ice**. It surrounds the continent during the winter months. Pack ice is between 300 miles (483 km) to 1,800 miles (2,897 km) wide.

Huge icebergs drift in Antarctic waters.

Name: ______________________ Date: ______________

Questions for Consideration

1. How much of Antarctica is covered with ice?

____

2. What is the average thickness of Antarctica's ice sheet?

____

3. What percent of the world's fresh water is in Antarctica's ice?

____

4. What is Antarctica's largest ice shelf?

____

5. How long was the largest recorded iceberg?

____

Matching

Match each description in the left column with the type of ice in the right column.

______	1. Moves by gravity	A. Ice Sheet
______	2. Made of seawater	B. Ice Shelf
______	3. On top of a land mass	C. Glacier
______	4. About ten percent appears above water	D. Iceberg
______	5. Surrounds Antarctica in the winter	E. Pack Ice
______	6. Is over two miles (3 km) thick in many places	
______	7. Attached to land, but floats on water	
______	8. Has about 90 percent of the world's ice	
______	9. Floats on water, but is not attached to land	
______	10. About ten percent of Antarctica's ice cover is this type	

DID YOU KNOW?

Antarctica's icebergs have not caused as much danger to ships as those in the northern Arctic region; there are no major shipping routes near Antarctica.

Antarctica's Animal Life

Clockwise from top right: Some of Antarctica's animals include skua, albatross, krill, and whales.

Antarctica's dry and bitterly cold climate limits its plant and animal life.

Most of Antarctica's plant life are simple, often single-cell organisms. Algae, bacteria, fungi, lichens, and mosses grow on Antarctica's few land outcroppings. At times, algae grows on the snow cover, creating green, yellow, or red patches on the snow.

Seaweed grows in most of the continent's coastal waters.

Only two flowering plants, the pearlwort and a flowering grass, grow south of the 60°S latitude.

Krill is the most important animal in Antarctica. It is a small shrimp-like animal that grows to approximately one inch (2.54 cm) long. Krill is important in the diet of the rest of the animal life in the region. Antarctica's fish, birds, seals, and whales all feed on krill. It is often considered to be Antarctica's major resource to the rest of the world.

Forty species of seabirds, including seven species of penguins, live on the continent. Penguins have oily feathers and a layer of fat to insulate them against the cold. Penguins cannot fly, but they are good swimmers and can dive deep into the water to obtain food. Penguins swim up to 25 miles (40 km) per hour and can jump as high as six feet (1.8 m).

Four species of albatross also live on the continent. The **albatross** is a bird whose body is about nine inches across; however, its wingspan often reaches more than 11 feet (3 m) from tip to tip.

Other seabirds living on the continent include a variety of gulls, skuas, and terns. They live mostly on the islands and in the coastal regions.

Six different species of seals live in Antarctica. The Weddell seal, named for James Weddell, an early explorer, lives farther south than any other species of seal. The Weddell seal uses a form of sonar to locate its food. It can stay underwater for up to an hour, and can dive to depths of 200 feet (61 m).

Seals were almost hunted to extinction for their fur and oil. Eventually, international laws were passed to protect them.

Seven species of whales spend part of their lives in Antarctic waters. One of these, the blue whale, is the largest creature on Earth. At one time, there were over 200,000 blue whales; today, there may be only 1,000. Like the seals, the whales are now protected by international law.

Eight species of dolphin are also found in the waters off Antarctica.

Name: ______________________________ Date: ______________

Questions for Consideration

1. What grows on Antarctica's snow, making green, yellow, or red patches?

   ____

2. What is considered to be Antarctica's major resource to the rest of the world?

   ____

3. How many species of penguins live in Antarctica?

   ____

4. What type of animal is an albatross?

   ____

5. What were once hunted almost to extinction for their fur and oil?

   ____

DID YOU KNOW?

Penguins feed underwater and do not know how to eat on land. Eating on land is a skill that some penguins in zoos learn.

For Further Research

Choose one of the unusual animals mentioned in the narrative with which you are less familiar. Use at least two sources to help you. Write a paragraph in the space below describing this animal.

____

____

____

____

____

____

____

____

Early Exploration of Antarctica

Two thousand years before the first human saw Antarctica, philosophers and astronomers believed it existed.

The ancient Greek philosopher Aristotle believed that a huge land had to be in the Southern Hemisphere to balance the then known land in the Northern Hemisphere. He named this unknown land *Antarktikos,* which meant "anti-arctic" or "opposite the arctic."

The Egyptian geographer Ptolemy believed that the earth was round and must have a large southern continent. He named this land *Terra Australis Incognita,* which meant a "southern, unknown land."

The first person to cross the Antarctic Circle was the British captain James Cook. The Antarctic Circle is the latitude of sixty-six degrees, thirty-three minutes south. It is the beginning of the southern frigid zone. During his 1773 voyage, Cook sailed around the continent but did not get close enough to see land. He did see many icebergs, and concluded that they would have come from land farther south.

In 1819 and 1820, Fabian Gottlieb von Bellingshausen, a Russian, led two expeditions to Antarctica. He was within sight of the mainland, only 20 miles (32 km) away, but did not realize his discovery.

The first person to set foot on the continent was an American. Captain John Davis arrived in 1821. Because Davis hunted seals, he was looking for a new location to hunt. However, he did not hunt there and soon returned to America.

Several expeditions from many nations continued throughout the rest of the nineteenth century. British explorer Edward Bransfield sighted the Antarctic Peninsula in 1820. In 1823, British sailor James Weddell explored the region. The Weddell Sea and a type of seal were both named for him.

French explorer Jules Dumont d'Urville discovered part of the Antarctic Peninsula, which he named "Terre Louis Philippe," in honor of the French King. American Charles Wilkes explored the ice coast, which was later named Wilkes Land in his honor. British explorer Sir James Clark Ross discovered the huge ice shelf that is now named for him. During the last part of the nineteenth century, whale- and seal-hunting crews explored much of the coastline.

In 1897, a Belgian expedition became trapped for over 13 months when their ship became iced in. Although they had not planned to stay, they became the first humans to spend the winter on the continent. The first expedition that had previously planned to stay throughout the winter was a British expedition in 1899.

Robert Falcon Scott and his men harnessed themselves to their loaded sleds. This was called "man-hauling."

Robert Falcon Scott led one of the most famous expeditions to the continent. Between 1901 and 1904, Scott and his men spent two winters in McMurdo Sound. Scott made the first attempt to reach the South Pole. He was not able to reach the Pole, but set a new record for traveling the farthest south.

Name: ______________________________ Date: ______________

Questions for Consideration

1. Who first used the name *Antarktikos*?

   ____

2. Who first used the name *Terra Australis Incognita*?

   ____

3. Who was the first person to cross the Antarctic Circle?

   ____

4. Who was the first person to set foot on Antarctica?

   ____

5. Who made the first attempt to reach the South Pole?

   ____

Name That Year

In the blank in front of each event, write the year the event took place.

_______ 1. Bransfield saw the Antarctic Peninsula.

_______ 2. The beginning of Scott's first expedition

_______ 3. Bellingshausen's first expedition

_______ 4. The first person set foot on Antarctica.

_______ 5. Cook's voyage

_______ 6. Weddell explored the region.

_______ 7. A Belgian expedition was trapped for 13 months.

_______ 8. The first expedition that had actually planned to stay throughout the winter

_______ 9. Bellingshausen's second expedition

_______ 10. Scott returned from his first attempt to reach the South Pole.

DID YOU KNOW?

One reason that people did not believe the theories of Aristotle and Ptolemy was because most people at that time thought the world was flat.

The Race to the South Pole

Roald Amundsen reached the South Pole on December 14, 1911.

Explorers competed to be the first to arrive at both the North Pole and the South Pole.

American Robert E. Peary reached the North Pole on April 6, 1909.

Robert F. Scott failed in his attempt to reach the South Pole during his 1901–1904 expedition.

Ernest Shackleton was a member of that expedition. In 1908, Shackleton returned with his own expedition; however, it failed because of a lack of food.

When Scott returned to Antarctica in 1910 for a second attempt to reach the South Pole, he found himself in a race with Norwegian Roald Amundsen.

In October, Scott and four of his men left their base on Ross Island and headed towards the Pole. They arrived at the Pole on January 17, 1912. They were bitterly disappointed to discover that Amundsen had been there five weeks before them.

Amundsen arrived at Antarctica in 1910 and began making preparations for the trip to the Pole. He established three deposits of food and supplies along part of the route he planned to take later.

On October 29, 1911, he and four men began their trip. They left the Bay of Whales on the Ross Ice Shelf just four days before Scott began his trip.

Part of Amundsen's success was his careful planning. He planned a shorter route than Scott. He also used dog teams and sleds to carry the men and supplies for the first part of the trip. This helped conserve the men's energy for the return trip.

Amundsen and his men arrived at the South Pole on December 14, 1911. They began their return trip three days later. The round trip to the Pole took 99 days and covered 1,860 miles (2,993 km).

When they arrived at the Pole, Scott and his men found a note from Amundsen. It said: "Dear Captain Scott, As you probably are the first to reach this area after us, I will ask you kindly to forward this letter to King Haakon [of Norway]. If you can use any of these articles left in the tent, please do not hesitate to do so. With kind regards, I wish you a safe return. Yours truly, Roald Amundsen."

Scott and his men left the following day, after doing some scientific investigations. All of them died on the return journey. Two of the men died of injuries. Scott and the other two men became trapped in a blizzard; they were only a few miles from their food supplies. They died from starvation and exposure to the bitter cold. Eight months later a search party found their tent and frozen bodies. Scott's last entry in his diary was: "... we are getting weaker, of course, and the end cannot be far. It seems a pity, but I do not think I can write more."

Name: ______________________ Date: ____________

Questions for Consideration

1. Who was the first man to reach the North Pole?

 ____

2. What was his nationality?

 ____

3. Who was the first man to reach the South Pole?

 ____

4. What was his nationality?

 ____

5. How many days did the successful trip to the South Pole and back take?

 ____

Time Line

Put a "1" in front of the first event to happen, and continue numbering the events in the order each occurred.

_____ 1. Shackleton returned with his own expedition.

_____ 2. Amundsen reached the South Pole.

_____ 3. A search party finds the bodies of Scott and his men.

_____ 4. Scott returned for his second attempt.

_____ 5. Scott's first expedition ends.

_____ 6. Peary reached the North Pole.

_____ 7. Scott and his men die in a blizzard.

_____ 8. Scott's first attempt to reach the South Pole begins.

_____ 9. Amundsen leaves a note for Scott.

_____ 10. Scott reached the South Pole.

DID YOU KNOW?

Today there is a scientific research station at the South Pole. It is named the Amundsen-Scott South Pole Station in honor of the first two men to lead expeditions to reach the Pole.

Shackleton and his 27 men spent many months drifting on an ice floe.

Ernest Shackleton

Ernest Shackleton (1874–1922) is one of Antarctica's most famous explorers. He was an Irishman and always had his men's loyalty.

Shackleton was a member of Robert F. Scott's first expedition to Antarctica in 1901–1904. In the spring, Scott, Dr. Edward Wilson, and Shackleton set out to discover the length of the Ross Ice Shelf.

The sled dogs died, and the men had to finish the trip hauling the sleds themselves. The men developed scurvy and had to return. Shackleton became too ill to travel, and the other two men had to put him on the sled to pull him back; he was forced to return to England against his will on a relief ship.

Shackleton began his own exploration in 1909 with a group of carefully selected men. They explored and conducted scientific experiments. They explored Mount Erebus, an active volcano. They also found a sample of coal from the mountain region. Since coal is made from plant material, it proved that Antarctica had at one time had a semitropical climate.

In October, three members of the expedition set out to reach the magnetic South Pole. They found it on January 18, 1909. By the end of their return trip, they had covered over 1,260 miles (2,028 km) on foot, hauling the sleds loaded with supplies and equipment.

At the same time that the group headed off to find the magnetic Pole, Shackleton and three men started out in a quest to be the first humans to ever reach the geographic South Pole. They crossed the Ross Ice Shelf and discovered the Beardmore Glacier. They reached the polar plateau but ran out of food and had to return before reaching the South Pole. They had been within 97 miles (156 km) of reaching it.

Shackleton and his men returned home in triumph, even though they did not reach the Pole. King Edward VII of England knighted Shackleton to honor him for his adventures and bravery.

Shackleton was disappointed to learn that Roald Amundsen had become the first person to reach the South Pole in 1911. In spite of his disappointment, Shackleton returned in 1914 to cross the entire continent by way of the Pole. His ship never reached the continent; it became trapped by the ice and sank ten months later. Shackleton and his 27 men spent many months drifting on an ice floe. When they reached Elephant Island in a lifeboat, they had not been on solid ground for 485 days. Shackleton and five volunteers sailed to a whaling station on South Georgia Island to get help. They returned to rescue the stranded men three months later.

Shackleton sailed on his third expedition to Antarctica in 1920. While on the ship, he suffered a heart attack and died, one month before his forty-eighth birthday. He was buried on South Georgia Island.

Name: ______________________________ Date: ______________

Questions for Consideration

1. What was Shackleton's nationality?

   ____

2. When did Shackleton begin his own exploration of Antarctica?

   ____

3. What did Shackleton discover that proved Antarctica had once had a semitropical climate?

   ____

4. How far was Shackleton from reaching the South Pole when he had to turn back?

   ____

5. Which king knighted Shackleton?

   ____

True or False?

Mark each of the following statements about Shackleton and his expedition with a plus sign (+) if it is true, and a minus sign (-) if it is false.

_____ 1. Shackleton is buried on South Georgia Island.

_____ 2. Three of his men arrived at the magnetic South Pole.

_____ 3. Shackleton was a member of Scott's first expedition.

_____ 4. Three of his men arrived at the South Pole.

_____ 5. Shackleton explored an active volcano.

_____ 6. Shackleton retired from exploration on his sixty-first birthday.

_____ 7. Shackleton discovered the Beardmore Glacier.

_____ 8 Shackleton experienced a series of earthquakes.

_____ 9. Shackleton had to be sent home from Scott's expedition when he contracted smallpox.

_____ 10. Shackleton discovered the Ross Ice Shelf.

DID YOU KNOW?

Scurvy is a disease caused by a lack of vitamin C. It can be prevented by eating vegetables or citrus fruits.

Later Exploration of Antarctica

Richard Byrd

After Norwegian explorer Roald Amundsen reached the South Pole in 1911, interest in the continent slowed; however, scientific explorations continued.

On May 9, 1926, American Richard Byrd became famous as the first person to fly over the North Pole.

In 1928, Australian Hubert Wilkins was the first person to fly over part of Antarctica. He later made several additional flights over the Antarctic Peninsula.

On November 2, 1929, Byrd and his crew of three men became the first to fly over the South Pole. Three days later, Amundsen, Italian Umberto Nobile, and American Lincoln Ellsworth flew over the Pole in a dirigible.

Byrd flew over the Pole again on November 29, 1929, and took many aerial photographs during this flight. He returned and took additional aerial photographs during four expeditions between 1933 and 1947. His photographs helped prove that Antarctica was a single continent.

In addition to Byrd's work, Britain, Australia, New Zealand, America, and Germany all sponsored additional photographic flights.

Between 1929 and 1950, many additional expeditions visited the continent. George Wilkins and Douglas Mawson of Australia, Hjalmar Riiser-Larsen of Norway, and Lincoln Ellsworth and Finn Ronne of the United States all headed major expeditions.

Ellsworth and Englishman Herbert Hollick-Kenyon made the first flight across most of the continent in November 1935. They flew 2,300 miles (3,701 km). Their plane ran out of fuel before reaching their final destination, however, and the two men had to walk for 22 days to return to their base.

The first to cross the entire continent by land were Englishman Vivian Fuchs and his expedition. Their 1958 journey took ninety-nine days.

In 1948, Australia built the first permanent observation station on the continent, and in 1955–1956, 12 nations set up 50 bases for scientific research. July 1, 1957, through December 31, 1958, was declared to be the International Geophysical Year (IGY). A major multinational research effort occurred throughout that year's time. By then, the emphasis had shifted from exploration to scientific research.

On December 1, 1959, 12 nations signed the Antarctic Treaty, which made the continent a non-military zone for scientific research.

Other historic events continued on the continent. A United States Navy airplane made the first landing at the South Pole in 1958. In 1990, a six-man dog-sled expedition traveled 3,700 miles (5,955 km) across the continent. In 1993, Norwegian Erling Kagge traveled alone and on foot 810 miles (1,304 km) across the continent to the South Pole.

Name: ______________________________ Date: ______________

Questions for Consideration

1. Who was the first person to fly over the South Pole?

____

2. What country built the first Antarctic observation station?

____

3. What did "IGY" stand for?

____

4. When was the Antarctic Treaty signed?

____

5. When did the first person cross Antarctica alone on foot to reach the South Pole?

____

Nationalities

Match each of the explorers in the left column with his correct nationality in the right column.

	Explorer		Nationality
______	1. Amundsen	A.	American
______	2. Byrd	B.	Australian
______	3. Ellsworth	C.	Danish
______	4. Fuchs	D.	English
______	5. Hollick-Kenyon	E.	Italian
______	6. Mawson	F.	Norwegian
______	7. Nobile		
______	8. Riiser-Larsen		
______	9. Ronne		
______	10. Wilkins		

DID YOU KNOW?

In 1935, the first woman set foot on Antarctica.

She was Caroline Mikkelsen, the wife of a whaling ship captain.

Antarctica's Conservation

During the early exploration of Antarctica, little thought was given to protecting its natural resources.

In the 1950s, the growing number of research stations began to concern environmentalists. The conservation of Antarctica's environment has now become a major concern among nations participating in research on the continent.

The buildup of waste began to become a concern on Antarctica.

Environmental groups such as Greenpeace and the World Wildlife Foundation began organizing campaigns to increase public awareness about conservation issues.

They argued against the increase of garbage and abandoned buildings left behind at the research centers. As these concerns increased, many nations began cleaning up dumps and shipping garbage and obsolete equipment back to the country operating each base.

Another major concern was raised about the construction of any new bases near animal breeding grounds. Most nations have agreed to carefully study the impact on the environment before beginning any construction.

Scientists have discovered several minerals including iron, copper, gold, and silver in Antarctica. So far, the minerals have not been found in quantities large enough to make it worthwhile to mine them. Oil and natural gas have also been discovered on the continent. Environmentalists are concerned that in the future some nations may try mining or drilling for these natural resources. Any mining or drilling would have a major impact on Antarctica's wildlife habitats.

In 1991, 31 nations signed the Madrid Protocol. This was an agreement that banned any oil and gas exploration in Antarctica for 50 years.

Another area of concern is the increasing number of tourists who visit the continent. From the 1960s to the present day, more tourists visit the continent each year. In recent years, thousands of tourists have visited the continent, traveling by ship. Many more fly over the continent.

In recent years, thousands of tourists have visited the continent, traveling by ship.

Since the tourists stay briefly, they have not had a major impact on the environment yet, but fears are that increasing numbers may have a negative effect.

Much of the scientific research that is conducted in Antarctica is done because of its unique ecology, atmosphere, and environment. These conditions must be protected so the research may continue. One plan discussed often is declaring the entire continent protected as a wildlife preserve and an international park.

Name: ______________________ Date: ______________

Questions for Consideration

1. What two organizations have worked to increase public awareness about Antarctica's conservation?

   ______________________ ______________________

2. When was the Madrid Protocol signed?

   ____

3. How many nations signed the Madrid Protocol?

   ____

4. For how many years did the Madrid Protocol ban oil exploration?

   ____

5. How do most tourists visit Antarctica each year?

   ____

Help the Environment

Write a letter to your senator explaining your opinion about the conservation of Antarctica's environment. Use your own paper if you need more room.

Dear Senator ______________________,

____

Sincerely,

____

DID YOU KNOW?

Between 1977 and 1980, over 11,000 passengers made about 45 sightseeing flights over Antarctica.

Scientific Research

Scientists from all over the world conduct research in Antarctica.

Antarctica has become a major site for scientific research. Much of the research cannot be done anywhere else.

In 1939, the United States Antarctic Service Expedition under Richard Byrd suggested the building of permanent research stations for scientific study. Two stations opened in 1941, but they were closed a year later because of World War II.

Other governments soon established stations to protect territory claims and conduct research.

During the International Geophysical Year (IGY), from July 1957 to December 1958, twelve nations agreed to cooperate on scientific research. More than 5,000 scientists worked in 49 stations. After the IGY ended, twelve nations agreed to continue cooperative research as part of the Antarctic Treaty.

Presently, during the summer, about 3,500 people conduct research. About 1,000 remain through the winter months. In the late 1990s, scientists from 17 nations operated 36 stations. The largest station is McMurdo.

Scientists study a variety of subjects. **Meteorologists** and **climatologists** study atmosphere and weather conditions. By digging through layers of ice, they can study the change of climate for thousands of years. They also have been studying the "ozone hole," which is a hole in the earth's protective ozone layer. The hole reappears each spring and lasts for several months.

Geologists are studying the land structures of the continent. They are also studying the movement of the plates of the earth's crust.

Biologists study responses of animals, and **botanists** study plants' reactions to extreme conditions.

Paleontologists study fossils. Antarctica has become a source of fossils that help trace the continent's history over tens of thousands of years. In 1991, scientists discovered the remains of a previously unknown dinosaur. It was a theropod over 25 feet (7.6 m) long. It lived in the early Jurassic period.

Glaciologists study the movements of layers of ice covering the continent. Other scientists put radio transmitters on icebergs to plot their movements. Some are studying the possibility of towing icebergs to dry regions as a source of fresh water.

Ecologists measure the impact of humans on the polar environment, and **psychologists** study the effects of the polar environment on humans.

The thin atmosphere allows **physicists** to study auroras, cosmic rays, and radio waves.

Bacteriologists study the behavior of bacteria and viruses in a cold, isolated environment.

Name: ________________________________ Date: ____________________

Questions for Consideration

1. When did the United States open its first research station in Antarctica?

____

2. How many nations joined together for research during the IGY?

____

3. About how many people do research in Antarctica each summer?

____

4. What type of unique dinosaur was discovered in Antarctica?

____

5. How do scientists plot the movements of icebergs?

____

Scientists

Match the scientists in the first column with the type of research they would do.

	Scientists		Research
________	1. Bacteriologists	A.	Animals
________	2. Biologists	B.	Atmosphere
________	3. Botanists	C.	Cosmic Rays
________	4. Ecologists	D.	Environment
________	5. Geologists	E.	Fossils
________	6. Glaciologists	F.	Human behavior
________	7. Meteorologists	G.	Land formations
________	8. Paleontologists	H.	Movements of layers of ice
________	9. Physicists	I.	Plants
________	10. Psychologists	J.	Viruses

DID YOU KNOW?

The McMurdo Station is a major supply depot for the other Antarctic research stations. Each year, thousands of tons of cargo arrive by air and sea, to be sent to the other camps. It has a population of over 1,000 in the summer and 180 in the winter.

Governing Antarctica

Based on early explorations, Argentina, Australia, Britain, Chile, France, New Zealand, and Norway have claimed territory in Antarctica.

Belgium, France, Japan, Russia, the United States, and South Africa have also done research on the continent, but have not made territorial claims.

The United States' policy is that all nations should have free access for peaceful pursuits, and it does not support any nation's claims.

After the cooperation of many nations during the International Geophysical Year, 12 nations agreed to extend cooperation.

Twelve nations signed the Antarctic Treaty on December 1, 1959, in Washington D.C. It went into effect in June 1961.

By 2000, 15 additional nations had joined the original member nations and another 17 nations agreed to its provisions.

The **Antarctic Treaty** had several major provisions:

- Antarctica shall be used for peaceful purposes only. It forbids any military maneuvers or the building of military bases and fortifications.
- Freedom of scientific investigations would continue.
- There shall be an exchange of scientific information and personnel.
- The treaty does not support or deny any claims to the continent.
- Nuclear testing and disposal of radioactive wastes are prohibited.
- There will be free access for observation and inspection.
- Personnel are under the jurisdiction of their sponsoring country.
- The treaty members will meet to continue reviewing the treaty and to settle disputes.

Many of the decisions of the treaty's member nations have dealt with conservation and protection of the continent's natural resources. Decisions have helped protect seals, managed commercial fishing by creating fishing zones, and established limits and bans on the hunting of some species.

Antarctica has some mineral and oil deposits. However, member nations had concerns about possible environmental threats that mining and drilling could bring. In 1991, the participating nations of the Antarctic Treaty agreed to avoid any mining activities for 50 years.

Name: ______________________________ Date: ______________

Questions for Consideration

1. How many nations have claimed territory in Antarctica?

____

2. How many nations have done research in Antarctica but have not made territorial claims?

____

3. How many nations signed the original Antarctic Treaty?

____

4. By 2000, how many additional nations signed the Antarctic Treaty?

____

5. For how many years did the 1991 agreement ban mining activities?

____

Treaty or Not?

If the following statements are part of the Antarctic Treaty, put a plus sign (+) in front of the statement; if the statement is not part of the treaty, put a minus sign (-) in front of the statement.

_____ 1. It supports some nations' claims on Antarctica territory.

_____ 2. It forbids nuclear testing.

_____ 3. It encourages freedom of observation.

_____ 4. It forbids military actions.

_____ 5. It allows for military fortifications.

_____ 6. It sets up a court system.

_____ 7. Its members will continue to review the treaty.

_____ 8. It encourages the exchange of scientific information.

_____ 9. Secret scientific investigation is encouraged.

_____ 10. Personnel are under its jurisdiction.

DID YOU KNOW?

Due to the Antarctic Treaty, ten percent of the world is now a nuclear-free, demilitarized zone.

Name: ______________________ Date: ____________

National Claims to Antarctica

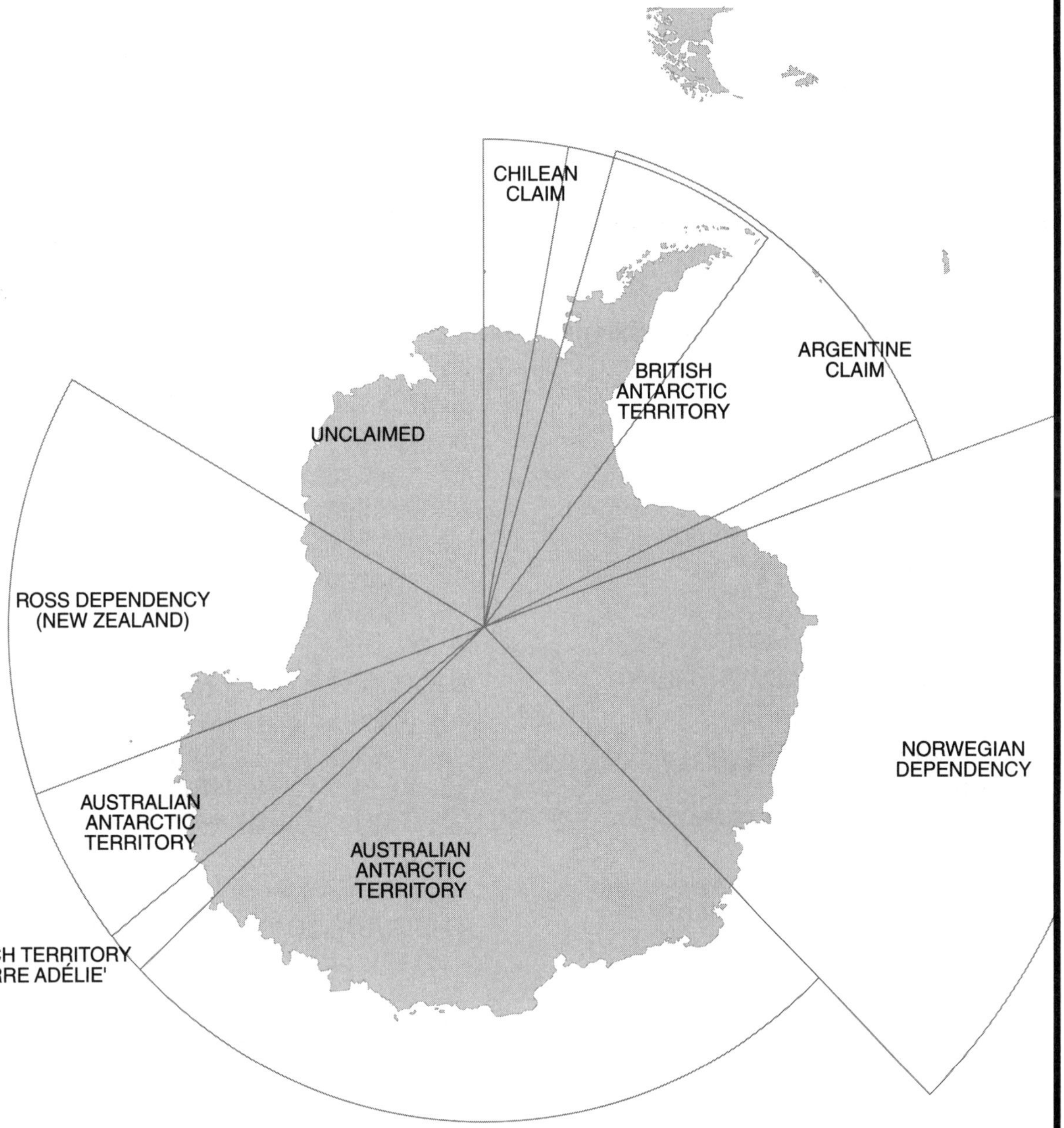

Answer Keys

THE CONTINENTS (page 3)
1. A large landmass completely or mostly surrounded by water
2. Just over 29%
3. Continental drift
4. Plate tectonics
5. Volcanoes and earthquakes

MAP PROJECT (page 3)
Teacher check map. Use the map on page 1 as a guide.

THE CONTINENT OF ANTARCTICA (page 6)
1. Opposite the Arctic
2. The Transantarctic Mountains
3. About 3,500
4. South America
5. Vinson Massif

MAP PROJECT (page 6)
Teacher check map.

ANTARCTICA'S CLIMATE (page 8)
1. -128.6°F (-89°C)
2. Commonwealth Bay
3. Around June 21
4. Less than 2 inches (5 cm)
5. 1985

TEMPERATURE (page 8)

1.	-150°C	6.	104°F
2.	0°C	7.	74°F
3.	30°C	8.	40°F
4.	50°C	9.	50°F
5.	95°C	10.	-133.6°F

ANTARCTICA'S ICE (page 10)
1. Over 95%
2. 7,090 feet (2,160 m)
3. 68%
4. Ross Ice Shelf
5. Over 200 miles (325 km)

MATCHING (page 10)

1. C	2. E	3. A
4. D	5. E	6. A
7. B	8. A	9. D
10. B		

ANTARCTICA'S PLANT AND ANIMAL LIFE (page 12)
1. Algae
2. Krill
3. Seven
4. Bird
5. Seals

EARLY EXPLORATION OF ANTARCTICA (page 14)
1. Aristotle
2. Ptolemy
3. Captain James Cook
4. Captain John Davis
5. Robert Falcon Scott

NAME THAT YEAR (page 14)

1. 1820	6. 1823
2. 1901	7. 1897
3. 1819	8. 1899
4. 1821	9. 1820
5. 1773	10. 1904

THE RACE TO THE SOUTH POLE (page 16)
1. Robert E. Peary
2. American
3. Roald Amundsen
4. Norwegian
5. 99

TIME LINE (page 16)

1. 3	6. 4
2. 6	7. 9
3. 10	8. 1
4. 5	9. 7
5. 2	10. 8

ERNEST SHACKLETON (page 18)

1. Irish
2. 1909
3. Coal
4. 97 miles (156 km)
5. Edward VII of England

TRUE OR FALSE (page 18)

1.	+	6.	-
2.	+	7.	+
3.	+	8.	-
4.	-	9.	-
5.	+	10.	-

LATER EXPLORATION OF ANTARCTICA (page 20)

1. Richard Byrd
2. Australia
3. International Geophysical Year
4. December 1, 1959
5. 1993

NATIONALITIES (page 20)

1.	F	6.	B
2.	A	7.	E
3.	A	8.	F
4.	D	9.	A
5.	D	10.	B

ANTARCTICA'S CONSERVATION (page 22)

1. Greenpeace, World Wildlife Foundation
2. 1991
3. 31
4. 50
5. By ship

SCIENTIFIC RESEARCH (page 24)

1. 1941
2. 12
3. 3,500
4. A theropod
5. By using radio transmitters

SCIENTISTS (page 24)

1.	J	6.	H
2.	A	7.	B
3.	I	8.	E
4.	D	9.	C
5.	G	10.	F

GOVERNING ANTARCTICA (page 26)

1. Seven
2. Six
3. 12
4. 15
5. 50

TREATY OR NOT? (page 26)

1.	-	6.	-
2.	+	7.	+
3.	+	8.	+
4.	+	9.	-
5.	-	10.	-

Bibliography

Baines, John. *Antarctica* (The Continents Series). Raintree/Steck Vaughn, 1997.

Billings, Henry, *Antarctica* (Enchantment of the World Series). Children's Press, 1994.

Fine, Jil. *The Shackleton Expedition.* Children's Press, 2002.

George, Michael. *Antarctica: Land of Endless Winter* (Life on Earth Series). Smart Apple Media, 2001.

Hackwell, W. John. *Desert of Ice: Life and Work in Antarctica.* Atheneum, 1991.

Harrington, Lyn. *The Polar Regions, Earth's Frontiers.* Thomas Nelson Inc., 1973.

Loves, June. *Antarctica: The Future,* Chelsea House Pub., 2002.

McMillian, Bruce. *Summer Ice: Life Along the Antarctica Peninsula.* Houghton Mifflin Co., 1995.

Nicholson, John. *The Cruelest Place on Earth: Stories from Antarctica* (True Stories Series). Allen and Unwin, 1997.

Petersen, David A. *Antarctica* (True Books: Continents Series). Children's Press, 1999.

Sayre, April Pulley. *Antarctica* (The Seven Continents Series) Twenty-First Century Books, 1998.

Schlensinger, Arthur. *Race for the South Pole: The Antarctica Challenge.* Cultural and Geographical Exploration Series). Chelsea House Pub., 1999.

Winckler, Susan; Rogers, Mary; Steger, Will., *Antarctica* (Our Endangered Planet Series). Lerner Publications Co., 1992

Woods, Michael. *Science on Ice: Research in the Antarctic.* Millbrook Press, 1995.